SYST
QUESTIONING
IN ACTION

101 Systemic Questions & Real-World Examples to
Enhanced Your Workplace Communication & Problem-
Solving Skills. A Must-Have Guide for Managers,
Consultants, & Coaches

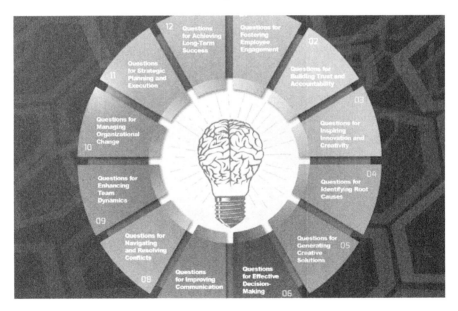

Erik Creed

Disclaimer

The author and publisher have made every effort to ensure that the information in this book is accurate and up-to-date. However, the author and publisher disclaim all warranties, express or implied, with respect to the accuracy or completeness of the information contained in this book. The author and publisher shall not be liable for any damages arising out of or in connection with the use of this book.

Table of content

Introduction 6

Purpose and Objectives of the Book 6

Chapter 1: Fundamentals of Systemic Questions 8

Key Concepts of Systemic Questions............................ 8

The Importance of a Systemic Perspective 9

Applications of Systemic Questions............................. 11

Chapter 2: Systemic Questions in Managerial Coaching.............. 13

Using Systemic Questions to Enhance Managerial Coaching ... 13

Understanding the Organizational System 14

Creating Meaningful Connections Through Questions.............. 16

Chapter 3: Systemic Questions in Change Management 18

A Systemic Approach to Change Management 18

Key Questions for Identifying Obstacles and Opportunities 20

Engaging Team Members Through Systemic Dialogue 21

Chapter 4: Systemic Questions in Organizational Analysis 23

Analyzing the Organization from a Systemic Perspective 23

Identifying Internal and External Dynamics............................. 24

Solving Complex Organizational Problems with Targeted
Questions 26

Chapter 5: Systemic Questions in Effective Leadership 28

The Role of Systemic Questions in Leadership 28

Building Successful Teams Through Systemic Thinking............ 29

Communicating the Vision Through the Language of Questions 30

Chapter 6: Systemic Questions in Organizational Consulting........ 32

The Organizational Consultant as a Change Facilitator............. 32

Using Systemic Questions for Diagnosis and Advising..............34

Collaborating with Clients in Solution Identification 35

Chapter 7: Practical Examples and Case Studies.........................37

In-Depth Analysis of Success Cases..37

Real-World Applications of Systemic Questions.......................38

Lessons Learned from Real-World Situations 39

Chapter 8: The 101 Best Systemic Questions and Their Answers .42

Question Series 1: Leadership and Motivation 42

Series of Questions 2: Problem Solving and Decision-Making ...49

Questions series 3: Effective Communication and Conflict
Resolution...55

Series of Questions 4: Change Management and Strategic
Development..61

Chapter 9: Case Studies and Real-Life Examples 67

Case Study 1: Transforming a Struggling Team Through Systemic
Leadership...67

Case Study 2: Resolving a Complex Organizational Crisis with
Systemic Questions 72

Case Study 3: Implementing Strategic Changes with Systemic
Consulting..77

Case Study 4: Creating a Successful Corporate Culture with
Systemic Leadership..81

Case Study 5: Implementing a Sustainable Growth Strategy
through Systemic Questions 83

Chapter 10: Developing Skills in Systemic Questions...................86

Tools and Techniques to Improve the Ability to Ask Systemic
Questions...86

Practical Exercises and Training Activities 87

Improving Your Systemic Thinking Skills....................................88

Conclusion...90

Summary of Key Concepts 90

Invitation to Apply What You've Learned 91

Additional Resources 93

Recommended Readings 93

Useful Websites and Online Resources 94

Index of Terms 97

Alphabetical list of key terms used in the book: 97

Introduction

Purpose and Objectives of the Book

In the contemporary era, marked by complexity and uncertainty in the organizational and managerial realms, your role as a manager, coach, or consultant has become crucial for the success of organizations. The ability to tackle complex challenges, lead change, and foster growth requires not only traditional skills but also a deep understanding of systemic dynamics that influence organizations. This book is here for you, to explore in detail the power of systemic questions as a fundamental tool in your practice. Systemic questions represent a revolutionary perspective in problem-solving and organizational dynamics management. They allow you to go beyond superficial solutions and address the root causes of issues, leading to profound and lasting changes.

Throughout this reading, we will together examine the fundamental principles of systemic questions, demonstrating how they can be applied in your specific contexts. We will discover how systemic thinking can enrich your managerial coaching, organizational consulting, and leadership, providing you with tools to better understand the complex dynamics that characterize modern organizations.

Each chapter of this book will focus on a specific aspect of systemic questions, providing practical examples, case studies, and applicable techniques. Real-life examples will illustrate how systemic questions can be successfully used to address complex business challenges and stimulate positive change. A key element of this book is the call to active practice. In addition to providing a theoretical understanding of systemic questions, we encourage you to practice the art of asking effective questions. Through practical exercises and training activities, you will develop specific skills to apply systemic questions in your professional contexts.

This guide aims to be your faithful companion as you aspire to become a successful manager, coach, or consultant in an increasingly complex and interconnected world. Understanding systemic questions and systemic thinking can represent a significant competitive advantage, enabling you to tackle challenges and opportunities with greater awareness and effectiveness. We invite you to explore the world of systemic questions and discover how they can enrich your professional practice and contribute to the success of your organizations and clients. Are you ready for a journey into the fascinating world of systemic thinking and the questions that fuel it?

Chapter 1: Fundamentals of Systemic Questions

Key Concepts of Systemic Questions

Systemic questions represent a revolutionary way to approach problems and manage dynamics within organizations. To fully grasp their potential, it's essential to have a solid foundation in the key concepts that underlie them. First and foremost, we need to understand the concept of interconnectedness and interdependence. Organizations are like intricate fabrics where each element is linked to the others. Systemic questions urge us to consider how each part influences and is influenced by the others. When tackling a problem, we must take into account how actions in one part of the organization can have ripple effects in other areas. But that's not all. Another fundamental aspect is circular thinking. While linear thinking seeks causes and effects sequentially, systemic thinking is circular. Systemic questions encourage us to explore how problems may result from cycles of interactions, feedback, and feedback loops. This circular approach enables us to uncover hidden dynamics and better understand complex situations. That's why systemic questions also prompt us to adopt a broad perspective. Instead of focusing solely on the obvious symptoms, they encourage us to delve into hidden roots. This perspective helps us avoid superficial solutions that may temporarily resolve symptoms but fail to address the underlying causes. Another important concept to consider is that of circular cause and effect. In organizations, cause-and-effect relationships are not always linear. Systemic questions help us identify how causes can become effects and vice versa. This is particularly useful when dealing with organizational change, as it allows us to understand how initial actions can generate unexpected outcomes later on. To complete the picture, systemic questions also promote objective observation. They challenge us to set aside biases and personal interpretations to look at facts and dynamics with fresh eyes. This objective approach is essential for identifying the real challenges and opportunities within the organization.

Finally, systemic questions encourage us to consider the long-term implications of actions and decisions. This awareness is crucial for the sustainability and long-term success of an organization. They challenge us to assess how today's choices can influence the future. These are some of the key concepts underlying systemic questions. Throughout the book, we will explore each of these concepts in detail, providing practical examples and tips on how to effectively apply them in your roles as a manager, coach, or consultant. Keep exploring this fascinating world, as gaining a deeper understanding of these concepts will make you a more effective and aware professional. With this solid foundation, you'll be ready to discover how systemic questions can transform your professional practice.

The Importance of a Systemic Perspective

Imagine being a manager, coach, or consultant faced with a complex problem within an organization. Without a systemic perspective, you might be tempted to address the problem in isolation, focusing your attention on a specific part of the organization or trying to solve only the visible symptoms of the problem. However, this limited perspective can lead to a series of challenges. For example, you might temporarily resolve the problem in one area, but by ignoring connections and interactions with other parts of the organization, you could inadvertently create new problems elsewhere. This is known as the "ping-pong ball effect," where the problem bounces from one part of the organization to another due to partial and isolated solutions.

A systemic perspective helps us avoid this kind of situation. It encourages us to view the organization as a complex and interconnected system in which each element has an impact on the others. This means that when we address a problem, we must consider the relationships and mutual influences among the various parts of the organization. Furthermore, it urges us to seek the root causes of problems rather than merely treating surface symptoms. A practical example can clarify this concept, giving you a clearer idea of what we're trying to convey. Imagine that a company is facing declining sales. A non-systemic approach might lead to immediate measures, such as downsizing the sales team or lowering product prices. However, a systemic perspective would prompt us to examine the entire value chain of the organization, including production operations, marketing strategy, product quality, and customer satisfaction.

This broader perspective might reveal that the problem doesn't solely reside in sales but is influenced by multiple factors, such as product quality or the effectiveness of marketing strategies. By addressing the problem systemically, you would have the opportunity to develop more comprehensive and lasting solutions that take into account all the interconnections and dynamics at play. This is a recurring theme in our guide and is fundamental to helping you think like a good manager or coach. You will fully understand the internal and external dynamics that influence the organization, avoiding partial solutions that serve only a few challenges.

Applications of Systemic Questions

Systemic questions offer a versatile and powerful approach to addressing a wide range of situations within organizations and beyond. This key concept is crucial for understanding how systemic questions can be practically applied in managerial, coaching, and consulting contexts. First, let's consider the application of systemic questions in the managerial context. Managers are responsible for making critical decisions that impact the organization's day-to-day operations and long-term success. These resources can be valuable tools for managers as they help consider the long-term implications of decisions and identify hidden relationships among different parts of the organization. For example, a manager might use systemic questions to examine how a decision about team structure can influence employee collaboration or customer satisfaction. In coaching, systemic questions are used to deepen coaches' understanding of their clients' issues and challenges. An experienced coach can ask questions that help the client explore the complex dynamics that may influence their situation. This may include questions about the client's professional network, cultural influences, or the impact of organizational decisions. Systemic questions open up new perspectives and allow the coach to delve deeper into the factors contributing to the client's situation.

In the field of organizational consulting, systemic questions are essential tools for exploring and understanding both internal and external dynamics of organizations. Consultants use systemic questions to conduct in-depth analyses and identify the root causes of problems. They can examine how organizational culture, structure, policies, or external influences may contribute to or hinder the organization's success. Systemic questions enable consultants to develop customized, context-oriented solutions rather than applying generic solutions. A key aspect of applying these questions is their ability to promote critical thinking and deep understanding. Regardless of the context, systemic questions encourage people to look beyond surface appearances and explore underlying dynamics. This means they can be applied to a wide range of challenges, including conflict resolution, change management, process optimization, leadership, and much more. The applications of systemic questions are broad and diverse, and their use can bring significant benefits in managerial, coaching, and consulting contexts. They are a powerfully flexible tool for exploring the complex dynamics that influence organizations and for developing targeted and sustainable solutions.

Chapter 2: Systemic Questions in Managerial Coaching

Using Systemic Questions to Enhance Managerial Coaching

Managerial coaching is a key activity for developing the skills of executives within an organization. Through coaching, managers can help their team members develop skills, overcome challenges, and achieve goals. The use of systemic questions in this context can bring significant advantages. First and foremost, managerial coaching with systemic questions encourages a holistic approach to analyzing challenges and opportunities. Instead of focusing exclusively on specific aspects or symptoms of a problem, managerial coaches can use questions to explore how the broader context can influence the situation. For example, if a team member is struggling with time management, managerial coaching can ask questions that delve into how the organization's structure or team expectations may contribute to time-related challenges. Systemic questions in managerial coaching also help identify interconnections and relationships within the organization. Managers can use questions that prompt the coach to reflect on how their actions may affect other team members or how group dynamics may impact their work. This helps promote a greater awareness of complex organizational dynamics. Another important aspect is the ability of systemic questions to reveal power dynamics and culture within the organization. Managers can use questions to explore how power structures influence decisions and how company culture can either support or hinder change. This can be particularly useful when it comes to promoting diversity and inclusion or addressing cultural challenges. Systemic questions can also be used to identify internal and external resources that can support the coaching process. A managerial coach can help the coach reflect on which connections, partnerships, or resources within or outside the organization can be used to support their professional development. Managerial coaching, with systemic questions, promotes a proactive approach to addressing challenges. Instead of reacting only to problems as they arise, the manager can use questions that push the coach to identify potential future challenges and develop plans to address them proactively. We could say that the use of systemic questions in managerial coaching enriches the executive's skill development process. These questions allow for an in-depth exploration of challenges, opportunities, and organizational dynamics, promoting greater awareness and better preparation for success.

Understanding the Organizational System

Understanding the organizational system is essential for any manager, coach, or consultant who aims to make a positive and lasting impact within an organization. An organization is much more than the sum of its parts; it's a complex system where each element is interconnected and interdependent. To effectively address challenges and drive change, it's essential to have a clear view of the organizational system as a whole. Systemic questions play a crucial role in this process. Firstly, they promote a broad perspective. Asking the team to reflect on the organizational system as a whole leads to the discovery of connections and relationships that might otherwise be overlooked. For example, a manager might ask questions like, "How do decisions made in our department affect other departments?" or "What are the dynamics that link internal processes to external clients?" Secondly, systemic questions encourage the consideration of feedback and feedback loops within the organization. This is particularly important when it comes to identifying the root causes of problems. Instead of stopping at a superficial answer to a problem, systemic questions can investigate how the problem itself might be a consequence of a cycle of past interactions. This approach can reveal more effective and lasting solutions. Another key aspect is the ability of systemic questions to identify patterns and trends within the organization. This can be useful for anticipating changes and developing proactive strategies. Questions might be oriented toward examining whether there are recurring patterns of behavior or issues that require special attention. Systemic questions can also reveal how values, culture, and power dynamics influence the organizational system. For example, questions like, "What values guide decisions within the organization?" or "How do power relationships affect the flow of information?" can be crucial in promoting the desired organizational culture and improving leadership dynamics. In the context of understanding the organizational system, they help identify levers for change. Once there's a clear view of the system, it's possible to identify where effective interventions can be made to bring about significant improvements. Questions can guide the search for improvement opportunities and help develop implementation strategies. Understanding the organizational system through the use of systemic questions is fundamental for effective management, coaching, and consulting. This approach promotes a comprehensive and interconnected view of the organization, helping to identify root causes, patterns, cultural dynamics, and levers for change.

Creating Meaningful Connections Through Questions

In the context of managerial coaching and organizational consulting, systemic questions play a fundamental role in "creating meaningful connections." This aspect focuses on the importance of using systemic questions to establish deep connections among team members and between different parts of the organization. Creating meaningful connections is crucial for fostering a collaborative work environment and a positive organizational climate. One of the most relevant applications of systemic questions in this context is using questions to explore interpersonal relationships. Questions can be oriented toward examining the quality of relationships among team members, understanding their dynamics, and identifying potential areas for improvement. For example, a question could be, "How do you perceive your ability to work effectively together as a team?" This type of question can bring to light any tensions or issues in relationships and create an opportunity to address them constructively. Systemic questions can also be used to promote awareness of group dynamics. They can help team members reflect on their interactions, the roles they play within the group, and how they can contribute to achieving common goals. For example, a question could be, "What roles do each of you perceive yourselves playing within the team?" This question can facilitate a discussion about task distribution and responsibilities. Additionally, systemic questions can be used to identify informal communication networks within the organization. They can explore how information flows between departments, who the key "information carriers" are, and if there are obstacles to effective communication. This understanding is essential for improving information transmission and knowledge sharing. But that's not all, as they can also be used to promote a sense of belonging and identification with the organization. Questions can be directed at exploring what it means to be part of the organization and how team members identify with it. For example, a question could be, "What makes being part of this organization special?" This type of question can strengthen the sense of community and belonging. The intention of this guide, therefore, is to make you understand how powerful systemic questions are for exploring and improving interpersonal relationships, group dynamics, organizational culture, internal communication, and a sense of belonging.

Chapter 3: Systemic Questions in Change Management

A Systemic Approach to Change Management

Change management represents one of the most challenging contexts for the application of systemic questions. Effectively addressing change within an organization requires not only an understanding of the dynamics of change but also the ability to consider the entire system at play. A systematic approach to change management begins with the awareness that a change in one area of the organization can have widespread impacts on other areas. Systemic questions prompt us to explore these connections. For example, if an organization is implementing a new computer system, systemic questions might include: "Which departments or teams will be affected by this change?" and "How can we ensure effective communication among all the teams involved?" These questions aim to identify the complex interactions that may arise as a result of the change. Another crucial aspect of the systemic approach to change management is considering resistance to change. Systemic questions can be used to explore the underlying reasons for this resistance and to identify influences that may come from different parts of the organization. This enables the development of more targeted strategies to address resistance. A question could be: "What are employees' concerns about this change, and what are the primary sources of these concerns?" This type of question promotes understanding of the individual and group dynamics that can influence reactions to change. Systemic questions can also help identify change levers within the organization. They can explore who the key players are who can promote and support the change. For example, a question could be: "Who are the key advocates within the organization who can positively influence the adoption of this change?" This type of question helps identify change champions and actively involve them in the change management process.

Furthermore, you can use these resources to monitor the progress of the change process, gather feedback from employees, and adapt strategies accordingly. A question could be: "What unexpected effects has the change had so far, and how can we proactively address them?" This way, you can promote flexibility and continuous adaptation during the change process. Systemic questions can also be used to promote an organizational culture that is open to change. They can explore how the organization handles change in general and how it can develop a mindset of continuous learning. Asking, "What processes does the organization have in place to learn from mistakes and constantly improve?" can encourage reflection on the organization's long-term adaptability. Our intention is to show you that a systematic approach to change management uses systemic questions to explore connections between different parts of the organization, address resistance to change, identify change levers, assess the impacts of change, and promote a culture open to change. This approach fosters more effective and sustainability-oriented change management in the context of modern organizations. By continuing to explore these applications of systemic questions, you will be able to develop advanced skills in change management.

Key Questions for Identifying Obstacles and Opportunities

When it comes to managing change within an organization, it's essential to clearly identify the obstacles that could slow down or hinder the change process, as well as the opportunities that can emerge from this process. Systemic questions provide a valuable framework for achieving this goal. One of the key questions for identifying obstacles is: "What are the main sources of resistance to change within the organization?" This question opens the door to identifying individuals, groups, or dynamics that may actively oppose the change. Identifying these resistances in a timely manner allows for the development of targeted strategies to address them. At the same time, it's important to ask, "What are the structural or procedural barriers that could hinder the adoption of change?" This type of question helps identify more tangible obstacles, such as outdated company policies or inadequate processes. Once identified, these obstacles can be addressed through the revision and updating of organizational structures and processes.

Regarding opportunities, a fundamental question is: "What positive outcomes could emerge from this change?" This question opens the door to a positive view of change, encouraging the identification of new opportunities, new approaches, or new business models that can result from the change process. It's a way to inspire innovation within the organization. Another crucial question is: "How can we capitalize on current resources and skills to maximize the opportunities?" This type of question promotes reflection on how to make the best use of existing resources within the organization to seize the opportunities generated by change. It can lead to creative strategies to optimize the use of available skills and resources.

Systemic questions also encourage consideration of the interactions between obstacles and opportunities. For example, you might ask, "Are there obstacles that could be transformed into opportunities?" This question promotes a more dynamic perspective, where obstacles are not necessarily insurmountable barriers but challenges that can lead to innovative solutions. However, it's important to also ask, "What strategies can we develop to maximize opportunities and overcome obstacles synergistically?" This type of question encourages holistic and strategic thinking, seeking ways to create synergies between actions aimed at seizing opportunities and those aimed at overcoming obstacles.

Engaging Team Members Through Systemic Dialogue

Actively engaging team members in a change process is essential for successful implementation. Systemic dialogue represents a powerful tool for creating an open environment where team members can express their opinions, concerns, and ideas. But how can you effectively engage the team through systemic dialogue?

First and foremost, it's important to create a climate of trust within the team. Individuals must feel free to express their thoughts without fear of judgment or retaliation. This requires open and understanding leadership that welcomes the input of each team member. A crucial aspect of systemic dialogue is active listening. Managers and leaders must demonstrate a genuine interest in what team members have to say. This means asking open-ended questions, seeking to understand others' perspectives, and responding empathetically. Active listening creates a sense of value for team members and makes them feel involved in the decision-making process.

Systemic dialogue also involves actively involving team members in defining goals and change strategies. Asking people to contribute to the design of change not only provides valuable ideas but also a sense of ownership of the process. When people feel involved in creating solutions, they are more likely to adhere to and support the change.

Systemic questions are a key tool for guiding systemic dialogue. For example, you might ask the team, "How do you think this change might impact our way of working?" or "What are your main concerns about this change?" These questions open up the discussion and encourage the team to reflect on the implications of the change for themselves and for the organization as a whole. It's also important to recognize and address differences of opinion constructively. Differences can lead to a better understanding of the complexities of change and potential challenges. Systemic dialogue includes managing differences through negotiation and finding solutions that take into account different perspectives.

Don't forget that systemic dialogue requires continuous follow-up. It's not a one-time conversation but an ongoing process of involving the team throughout the change. This involves constant communication, monitoring developments, and adapting strategies based on feedback and new information. Engaging team members through systemic dialogue is crucial for effective change management. It requires trust, active listening, active involvement in change design, and the use of systemic questions to guide dialogue. Managing differences constructively and maintaining an ongoing communication process are key elements in successfully engaging the team in the organizational change process.

Chapter 4: Systemic Questions in Organizational Analysis

Analyzing the Organization from a Systemic Perspective

Analyzing the organization from a systemic perspective is a deep process aimed at understanding the complexity of organizational dynamics. To do this successfully, it's essential to adopt a holistic approach that goes beyond merely observing individual parts. Instead, it involves looking at the organization as a whole, as an interconnected system of elements that mutually influence overall functioning.

A crucial aspect of systemic analysis is the consideration of interconnections. Every component or department within an organization is somehow linked to others. For example, a decision made by the human resources department can directly impact productivity in another department. These interconnections can be obvious or hidden but are essential for understanding how the organization functions as a whole. Systemic analysis also requires identifying patterns of organizational behavior. These patterns can emerge from cycles of interactions, feedback, and decision-making processes. Recognizing these patterns can help predict future dynamics and adopt more effective strategies. An essential element of systemic analysis is identifying change levers. These are areas where interventions can be made to positively influence the organization. Systemic questions play a crucial role in this process as they help identify change levers through in-depth inquiry. For example, you might ask, "What factors are contributing to this problem?" or "Where can we intervene to improve overall efficiency?" Systemic analysis also requires special attention to organizational culture. Culture profoundly influences the behavior of organization members and can be a driving force or a barrier to change. Understanding organizational culture through dialogue and systemic questions is essential for effectively guiding change.

This operation requires the adoption of a temporal perspective. It's not just about understanding the organization in the present moment but also examining its development over time. This may involve analyzing historical data, identifying trends, and evaluating possible future developments. Therefore, analyzing an organization from a systemic perspective is a complex but essential process for fully understanding organizational dynamics.

Identifying Internal and External Dynamics

In the process of systematically analyzing organizations, it's crucial to recognize and understand both internal and external dynamics that influence overall functioning. This approach allows for a comprehensive view of the organization and its interactions with the surrounding environment. First, let's focus on internal dynamics. These are the forces, relationships, and processes within the organization itself. Systemic questions can be powerful tools for exploring these dynamics. For example, you might ask, "What are the key roles within the organization, and how do they interact with each other?" or "What are the major decision-making processes, and how do they impact workflow?" Recognizing internal dynamics is essential for improving operational efficiency and collaboration within the organization. This may involve identifying any inefficiencies, conflicts, or obstacles that hinder the achievement of goals. In addition to internal dynamics, it's equally important to examine external dynamics. These include factors such as the market, competition, economic trends, government regulations, and social dynamics. Organizations do not exist in a vacuum but are profoundly influenced by what happens in the surrounding environment.

Systemic questions can be used to explore how these external dynamics can impact the organization. For example, you might ask, "What market trends could influence our business strategy?" or "How are government regulations changing, and what are the implications for our operations?" Identifying external dynamics is crucial for adapting to changes in the environment and identifying growth opportunities. This enables the organization to develop relevant and future-oriented strategies and action plans.

A crucial aspect of systemic analysis is recognizing the interactions between internal and external dynamics. These interactions can be complex and nuanced but significantly influence organizational behavior. An example could be how internal dynamics, such as corporate culture, influence an organization's ability to adapt to external changes, such as new government regulations. Identifying internal and external dynamics is essential for fully understanding the context in which an organization operates. Systemic questions provide an effective tool for exploring these dynamics and revealing the complex interactions between them. This approach enables the organization to develop an informed and future-oriented strategy, adapting to the challenges and opportunities in its environment.

Solving Complex Organizational Problems with Targeted Questions

Organizations, regardless of their size or industry, regularly face complex problems. These problems can range from managing internal conflicts to defining competitive strategies, from planning organizational change to resolving daily operational challenges. Addressing such problems requires a systemically oriented perspective and the use of targeted questions. Systemic questions offer a structured and focused approach to tackling complex organizational problems. Rather than addressing only the obvious symptoms, these questions prompt exploration of hidden dynamics and interconnections among various elements of the organization. For example, you might ask, "What are the underlying causes of internal conflicts?" or "How do management decisions made at the top impact day-to-day workflow?"

Solving complex organizational problems also requires careful analysis of cause-and-effect relationships. Systemic questions are effective tools for identifying how different actions and decisions may influence each other. This is particularly relevant when trying to predict the consequences of decisions or dealing with situations where solutions may have unexpected impacts. For example, you might ask, "What could be the ripple effects of this decision?" or "How might initial actions affect long-term outcomes?"

Another crucial aspect of addressing complex problems is the ability to define clear and measurable objectives. Systemic questions can help define objectives that take into account the complex dynamics of the organization. For example, you might ask, "What specific outcomes are we trying to achieve, and how can we measure them effectively?" or "What metrics can capture the long-term success of our initiatives?"

Solving complex organizational problems requires active engagement of various stakeholders within the organization. Systemic questions can facilitate dialogue and collaboration among team members, promoting a shared understanding of problems and solutions. For example, you might ask, "How can we involve employees in this decision-making process?" or "What are the perspectives of different stakeholders, and how can we take them into consideration?"

Chapter 5: Systemic Questions in Effective Leadership

The Role of Systemic Questions in Leadership

Effective leadership in a complex business context requires a set of skills and competencies. In addition to traditional management and communication skills, successful leaders can apply systemic thinking and systemic questions to their leadership. A leader who uses systemic questions can consider the organization as a whole, rather than focusing solely on isolated parts. This means having a complete view of the interconnections between various functions and departments of the organization. For example, a leader might ask, "How do decisions made in our department influence other teams?" or "What are the long-term implications of our actions on the entire organization?" Systemic questions allow leaders to explore hidden dynamics and underlying causes of problems. Rather than addressing only the obvious symptoms, a leader can dig deeper to identify the root causes of issues. This is particularly useful when dealing with complex situations or addressing persistent challenges. A leader might ask, "What are the deep-seated causes of our current problems?" or "How can we address these issues in a lasting way?"

Furthermore, systemic questions can help leaders make more informed decisions. When facing crucial decisions, a leader can use targeted questions to consider the potential long-term consequences and complex interactions that may occur. For example, they might ask, "What chain reactions could result from this decision?" or "How will this choice affect our overall strategy?" An important aspect of effective leadership is the ability to engage and inspire team members. Systemic questions can be effective tools for involving employees, asking them to actively contribute to problem-solving and share their perspectives. This promotes a sense of participation and responsibility within the team. Systemic questions play a fundamental role in effective leadership. Leaders who adopt this perspective are better able to understand the organization as a whole, address the underlying causes of problems, and make more informed decisions. Additionally, they can engage and inspire their team members, creating a collaborative and results-oriented work environment. By using systemic questions, leaders can successfully tackle the complex challenges of the contemporary business world and guide their organizations to long-term success.

Building Successful Teams Through Systemic Thinking

Leaders who adopt a systemic perspective understand the importance of building cohesive and successful teams. However, achieving this goal goes beyond simply selecting talented individuals. It requires a deep understanding of group dynamics, interactions among team members, and how the team integrates into the organization as a whole. Systemic questions are powerful tools for exploring these dynamics. For example, a leader might ask, "How do the personalities and skills of team members integrate to maximize overall effectiveness?" or "What group dynamics can hinder or facilitate our success?" A crucial aspect of building successful teams is the ability to manage conflicts constructively. Leaders who use systemic questions can analyze the root causes of conflicts and seek solutions that address the underlying problems rather than just the visible symptoms. They can ask, "What are the underlying causes of conflicts within the team?" or "How can we promote a culture of open and respectful communication?"

Furthermore, systemic questions can help leaders create an inclusive and collaborative work environment. By asking team members to share their perspectives and actively contribute to discussions, leaders promote a sense of participation and belonging. A leader can ask, "How can we value diverse perspectives within our team?" or "What practices can foster collaboration and innovation within the group?" By doing so, the leader can continually assess the team's effectiveness and make changes when necessary. In conclusion, building successful teams requires a deep understanding of group dynamics and organizational interactions. Leaders who use systemic questions can effectively explore these dynamics, manage conflicts constructively, create an inclusive work environment, and continually assess the team's effectiveness. Using this systemic perspective, they can guide their teams toward successful outcomes and contribute to achieving organizational goals.

Communicating the Vision Through the Language of Questions

In the context of effective leadership, communicating the vision is one of the crucial skills for inspiring and guiding a team toward success. Systemic questions can play a significant role in communicating a vision engagingly and clearly. To better understand how systemic questions can be used in this context, let's consider an example. Imagine a leader who wants to communicate a new vision for the organization's future. Instead of stating the vision outright, the leader could start with an open-ended question like, "How do you envision the organization's future five years from now?" This question opens up space for active participation from team members, encouraging them to express their visions and expectations.

Next, the leader could ask specific questions to further explore the vision with the team. For example, they might ask, "What are the key obstacles we need to overcome to realize this vision?" or "What concrete actions can we take today to move closer to this future vision?" These questions help translate the vision into tangible actions and concrete goals. Furthermore, systemic questions can promote open communication within the team. A leader might ask, "What are your thoughts and concerns about this new vision?" or "How can we ensure that everyone on the team has a say in its realization?" These questions encourage the sharing of perspectives and opinions, helping to prevent misunderstandings and resistance. Questions are also essential for continually assessing alignment between the vision and the team's actions. The leader can ask, "What are we doing to move closer to realizing the vision?" or "Are we moving in the desired direction, or are there signs that we need to adjust our strategy?" These questions help keep the focus on the vision and ensure that the team stays on the right track.

Chapter 6: Systemic Questions in Organizational Consulting

The Organizational Consultant as a Change Facilitator

In the context of organizational consulting, the role of a change facilitator is of paramount importance. The consultant is not merely an expert offering pre-packaged solutions but a strategic partner guiding the organization through the change process. Systemic questions emerge as a valuable tool for fulfilling this role effectively. An organizational consultant who adopts a systemic perspective focuses first on observing and understanding the organization as a whole, rather than having a fragmented view. They use open and incisive questions to explore the structure, dynamics, and relationships within the organization itself. For example, they might ask, "How are various departments interconnected within the organization?" or "What are the key interactions among the management team members?" These questions compel the organization to examine itself from a broader perspective and identify often-overlooked connections and interdependencies.

Furthermore, an organizational consultant who uses systemic questions can stimulate critical reflection within the organization. They ask questions that challenge the status quo and encourage thinking outside the box. They might inquire, "What are our entrenched beliefs about our market approach, and are they still valid?" or "What are the presumed causes of the problems we are facing, and are they based on concrete data?" These questions question assumptions and established habits, paving the way for new perspectives and innovative solutions.

The organizational consultant might also ask, "How do you envision the future of the organization, and what roles would you like to play in this transformation?" or "What are your primary concerns about this change, and how can we address them together?" These questions promote active employee engagement and foster a sense of ownership in the change process. This figure, utilizing systemic questions, is also capable of continually assessing the impact of change on the organization. They might ask questions like, "What are the signs that the change is succeeding?" or "Are there areas where the change is meeting resistance, and what can we do to address them?" These questions allow for real-time monitoring and adaptation of the change strategy.

We could say, then, that as a change facilitator, the organizational consultant can fully leverage the potential of systemic questions to guide the organization through complex change processes. These questions help gain a deeper understanding of the organization as a whole, encourage critical reflection, actively engage organization members, and provide an ever-evolving picture of the impact of change. In this way, systemic questions become a valuable tool in the toolkit of the modern organizational consultant, contributing to the success and sustainability of the organization itself.

Using Systemic Questions for Diagnosis and Advising

The use of systemic questions by an organizational consultant for diagnosis and advising is a crucial aspect of their work. This approach allows the consultant to gain an in-depth understanding of issues and dynamics within the organization, paving the way for targeted advice and effective solutions. One of the initial phases of the consulting process is information gathering and understanding the context. The consultant may start by asking questions like, "What are the most pressing challenges the organization is currently facing?" or "What are the evident symptoms of the problems you wish to address?" These initial questions help the consultant identify critical areas to focus on and understand the bigger picture. Subsequently, the consultant can use systemic questions to analyze the organizational structure and internal dynamics. They might inquire, "What are the key decision-making processes within the organization?" or "How is information and communication managed between departments?" These questions help identify possible inefficiencies or blockages in internal operations.

Another important dimension is the analysis of relationships and interactions among organization members. Systemic questions allow the consultant to explore how people communicate, collaborate, and handle conflicts. They might ask, "What are the primary communication channels within the management team?" or "How are conflicts among employees addressed?" These questions reveal interpersonal dynamics that can impact overall organizational functioning. Once detailed information has been gathered, the consultant can move on to the diagnosis and advising phase. Based on the responses to systemic questions and their understanding of the situation, they can develop targeted recommendations.

For example, if it becomes evident that the main problems stem from a lack of communication between departments, the consultant might suggest a plan to improve transparency and collaboration.

It's important to emphasize that systemic questions are not used in isolation but integrate into the entire consulting process. They are employed flexibly and adapted to the organization's specific situation. Additionally, the consultant must be skilled at creating an open and collaborative environment in which people feel comfortable responding to questions and actively participating in the change process. Ultimately, the use of systemic questions by an organizational consultant is a key element in accurately diagnosing issues and providing effective advice. This approach allows for a comprehensive overview of the organization, including challenges, internal dynamics, and interpersonal relationships. With this in-depth understanding, the consultant can develop tailored solutions that contribute to the organization's improvement and transformation.

Collaborating with Clients in Solution Identification

Collaborating with clients in solution identification is a crucial step in the work of an organizational consultant. In this phase, the consultant uses systemic questions to actively involve clients in the decision-making process and solution definition. This collaboration is essential to ensure that the proposed solutions are aligned with the needs and perspectives of key stakeholders within the organization.

The consultant can start this phase by asking clients about the outcomes they wish to achieve and the objectives they aim to reach. These initial questions help establish a clear framework of clients' expectations and priorities. For example, they might inquire, "What are your main goals for this consulting process?" or "What results do you expect to achieve?". Subsequently, the consultant can use systemic questions to explore clients' ideas and perspectives on the current situation and potential solutions. They might ask, "What do you believe needs to change within the organization to achieve your goals?" or "What are your thoughts on addressing the identified problems?". During this collaborative process, the consultant must listen attentively and show empathy toward clients' opinions and concerns. They must create an environment where clients feel free to express their views and contribute to the decision-making process. This active client engagement not only increases the likelihood of successful proposed solutions but also fosters a sense of ownership and commitment to change within the organization.

An important aspect of this phase is the creation of a shared action plan. Using the information gathered through systemic questions and collaboration with clients, the consultant can develop a detailed plan that outlines the actions to be taken, the required resources, and the implementation timelines. This plan should be constructed together with clients so that everyone is fully involved and committed to the process. Collaborating with clients in solution identification is thus an essential step in the work of an organizational consultant. Systemic questions are powerful tools for engaging clients, collecting valuable information, and creating tailored solutions. This approach not only enhances the quality of proposed solutions but also promotes a sense of responsibility and engagement among clients themselves.

Chapter 7: Practical Examples and Case Studies

In-Depth Analysis of Success Cases

A detailed analysis of success cases represents a fundamental exploration to fully understand how systemic questions can positively influence the performance of organizations. In this chapter, we will explore some success stories where the use of systemic questions has led to significant and sustainable results. One of the most well-known success cases involves a manufacturing company facing a series of challenges related to production and resource management. Initially, the company had sought isolated solutions to address each of the challenges, but the results were unsatisfactory. It was only when they adopted a systemic approach, asking questions that explored the interconnections between various issues, that they began to see significant improvements. Systemic questions pushed them to consider how decisions made in one area of the company could affect other areas. For example, they asked, "How do our resource management decisions impact the quality of the final product?" and "How can changes in the supply chain affect our operational efficiency?" These questions led them to reconsider their strategies on a broader scale, taking into account the interconnections between various aspects of their business.

Another interesting case involves an elementary school facing issues of low academic performance and student discomfort. Instead of seeking superficial solutions such as implementing new teaching programs, the school's leadership team started asking systemic questions. These industry experts examined how dynamics within the school could influence student well-being and learning. Systemic questions led them to consider the relationships between teachers, students, and parents, as well as the physical learning environment. They asked, "How does parental involvement affect student motivation?" and "How can the school's architecture either facilitate or hinder learning?" These questions prompted them to implement changes that improved the learning environment and relationships within the school, resulting in increased academic achievement and student well-being.

These are just two examples of how in-depth analysis of success cases can illustrate the potential of systemic questions in transforming organizations. In both cases, the systemic approach led to positive results because it allowed exploration of the complex interconnections between various elements at play. These stories demonstrate that systemic questions are not merely a theoretical concept but a concrete practice that can lead to real and significant changes in different organizational contexts.

Real-World Applications of Systemic Questions

Real-world applications of systemic questions provide a more detailed framework of how this approach can be successfully implemented in various organizational contexts. Let's consider a concrete example to illustrate the effectiveness of systemic questions in a technology company.

In this company, there had been a decline in productivity and increasing dissatisfaction among employees. Initially, management had sought isolated solutions, such as introducing bonuses or reducing working hours. However, the problems persisted. It was only when a systemic questions expert was brought in that significant progress began to be made. The consultant started asking questions that pushed the company to examine internal dynamics more deeply. For instance, they asked, "How are incentive policies affecting collaboration among employees?" and "How is the organizational structure hindering innovation?" These questions led to a broader reflection on the company's operations and relationships between various departments. What emerged was that the corporate culture had become overly focused on financial results, at the expense of collaboration and creativity. This discovery prompted the company to revise its culture and promote greater dialogue and idea-sharing among employees. Additionally, changes were made to the organizational structure to facilitate inter-departmental collaboration. Over time, the company saw an increase in productivity and an improvement in the organizational climate. Employees felt valued and began contributing more significantly to innovation and the company's success.

This case represents a tangible example of how systemic questions can be effectively applied to address complex issues within an organization. Rather than focusing solely on obvious symptoms, systemic questions led to the discovery of underlying dynamics and the creation of targeted and sustainable solutions. This is just one of many real-world cases that demonstrate the value of systemic questions in transforming organizations. Real-world applications highlight how the systemic approach can lead to significant results, promoting a deeper understanding of organizational dynamics and driving positive change.

Lessons Learned from Real-World Situations

Lessons learned from real-world situations offer valuable insights into the power of systemic questions in an organizational context. Let's examine another concrete situation to highlight the lessons that emerged from the application of this approach.

In a manufacturing company, there was a decline in product quality and an increase in customer complaints. Initially, the company had reacted by trying to identify production and quality control issues. However, the problems persisted and were spreading systematically throughout the company. An expert consultant in systemic questions was tasked with investigating the situation more thoroughly. They began to explore internal and external dynamics of the company through a series of targeted questions. For example, they asked, "How does the corporate culture influence employees' perception of quality?" and "What role do interactions between departments play in the emergence of problems?"

Through these questions, it emerged that the corporate culture had become centered on mass production and speed at the expense of quality and attention to detail. Furthermore, divisions between departments had become obstacles to communication and information sharing. These factors had contributed to the decline in product quality.

The consultant then collaborated with company leadership to promote a cultural shift that placed quality at the forefront. Measures were introduced to improve collaboration between departments and encourage open communication. Additionally, more rigorous quality monitoring systems were implemented. Over time, the company witnessed a significant improvement in product quality and a reduction in customer complaints. Employees felt engaged in the change process and embraced the new quality-oriented corporate culture. The lessons that emerge from this real-world situation are multifaceted. Firstly, it highlights the importance of considering the organization as a whole rather than focusing solely on specific areas. Systemic questions allowed for the detection of internal and external dynamics that influenced the overall situation. Secondly, this situation underscores the need for change-oriented leadership that is willing to critically examine corporate culture and make significant changes when necessary.

Finally, it illustrates how systemic questions can be effectively used to promote organizational change, leading to measurable and sustainable improvements. These lessons learned from real-world situations emphasize the relevance and effectiveness of systemic questions in analyzing and resolving organizational problems. They demonstrate how this approach can significantly contribute to the success and sustainability of organizations in an increasingly complex business environment.

Chapter 8: The 101 Best Systemic Questions and Their Answers

Question Series 1: Leadership and Motivation

Subcategory: Questions to Foster Employee Engagement

Employee engagement is the cornerstone of a motivated and productive team. These eight questions will help you connect with your team on a deeper level, understand their needs and aspirations, and create an environment in which they are engaged and enthusiastic.

Question 1: "What aspects of your job do you find most fulfilling, and how can we incorporate more of these elements into your role?"

Result 1: By asking this question, you open the door to discovering what truly motivates your employees. Their answers will guide you in customizing their roles to align with their passions and strengths, ultimately increasing engagement and job satisfaction.

Question 2: "Can you share a recent accomplishment or project where you felt particularly motivated and engaged? What contributed to that feeling?"

Result 2: This question encourages employees to reflect on moments of high engagement, providing valuable insights into the conditions and tasks that drive their motivation. Use this information to replicate such conditions when assigning future projects.

Question 3: "Are there specific skills or talents you possess that you believe are underutilized in your current role? How can we leverage these talents more effectively?"

Result 3: Employees often have hidden talents or skills that can benefit the organization if utilized correctly. Identifying and harnessing these talents not only increases engagement but also enhances the overall skill set of your team.

Question 4: "In your opinion, what is the most significant contribution you have made to the team or organization so far? How did it make you feel?"

Result 4: Recognizing and celebrating past contributions can boost an employee's sense of accomplishment and motivation. Use this question to acknowledge their value and encourage future contributions.

Question 5: "What challenges or obstacles do you encounter in your daily activities, and how can we support you in overcoming them?"

Result 5: Employee engagement often diminishes when obstacles compromise productivity. By actively addressing these challenges and providing support, you demonstrate your commitment to their success and well-being.

Question 6: "What additional training or resources do you believe would help you excel in your role and contribute more effectively to the team's success?"

Result 6: This question allows employees to take responsibility for their own professional development. Providing the requested resources or training not only improves their skills but also boosts their motivation.

Question 7: "What role do you envision for yourself in the team's future growth and success? How can we help you achieve this vision?"

Result 7: Encouraging employees to envision their future within the team fosters a sense of belonging and commitment. Your support in helping them realize their aspirations strengthens their commitment.

Question 8: "What suggestions do you have for improving our team's dynamics and collaboration? How can we create a more engaging and cohesive work environment?"

Result 8: Employees often have valuable insights on how to enhance teamwork and collaboration. Implementing their suggestions shows that their opinions matter, promoting a more engaging work environment.

By incorporating these questions and actively listening to your team's responses, you will not only foster employee engagement but also build stronger and more motivated teams aligned with your organization's goals. These questions are powerful tools in your leadership arsenal, enabling you to create a work environment where every team member feels valued and engaged.

Subcategory: Questions to Build Trust and Accountability

Building trust and promoting accountability are essential for effective leadership. These eight questions will guide you in creating a culture of trust within your team, where every member feels responsible and appreciated.

Question 1: "What actions or behaviors do you consider essential for building trust within our team, and how can we collectively ensure they are consistently practiced?"

Result 1: This question encourages team members to define the behaviors and actions that contribute to trust. Collaboratively establishing these principles ensures that everyone is on the same page regarding trust-building expectations.

Question 2: "Can you share an experience from your past where trust played a crucial role in achieving a common goal? What lessons can we learn from that experience?"
Result 2: Reflecting on past experiences, your team can identify real-life examples of the impact of trust. Drawing lessons from these experiences reinforces the importance of trust and accountability in achieving shared goals.

Question 3: "What do you believe are the main obstacles to open and honest communication within our team, and how can we address them to improve transparency and trust?"
Result 3: Identifying communication barriers helps pinpoint areas where trust might be lacking. Addressing these obstacles promotes transparent and open dialogue, essential for building trust.

Question 4: "How can we ensure that every team member feels heard and respected during discussions and decision-making processes?"
Result 4: Valuing each team member's contribution and ensuring their voices are heard fosters a sense of respect and inclusion. Implementing practices to achieve this goal demonstrates your commitment to trust and accountability.

Question 5: "What steps can we take to hold ourselves mutually accountable for our commitments and actions? How can we create an environment where accountability is valued?"

Result 5: Accountability should be a shared responsibility. This question invites team members to propose mechanisms for holding themselves and their colleagues accountable, emphasizing its importance.

Question 6: "How can we promote transparency regarding our individual and collective goals, ensuring that everyone understands their roles and responsibilities?"
Result 6: Clear goal definition and role clarification are vital for trust and accountability. Explore ways to make goals visible and easily accessible, ensuring that everyone knows their role in achieving them.

Question 7: "What can we do to create a safe space for acknowledging mistakes and learning from them? How can we turn obstacles into growth opportunities?"
Result 7: Mistakes are inevitable but can serve as valuable learning experiences. Creating a culture where mistakes are acknowledged and used as learning opportunities encourages accountability and trust.

Question 8: "How can we celebrate and recognize the achievements and contributions of each team member? What can we do to show appreciation and build a culture of recognition?"
Result 8: Recognizing and celebrating achievements strengthens trust and accountability. Discuss ways to ensure that each team member's contributions are acknowledged and appreciated.

By incorporating these questions into your leadership approach and actively engaging with your team's responses, you will be well on your way to building a culture of trust and accountability. These questions allow you to collaboratively establish trust-building practices and accountability mechanisms, promoting a stronger and more cohesive team.

Subcategory: Questions to Inspire Innovation and Creativity

Inspiring innovation and creativity is essential for progress and growth. These eight questions will help you cultivate an environment that encourages new ideas and creative solutions within your team.

Question 1: "What unconventional approaches or out-of-the-box ideas can we explore to address this problem?"
Result 1: Embracing unconventional thinking can lead to revolutionary solutions. Encourage brainstorming sessions to generate unique ideas.

Question 2: "How could we adapt successful strategies from other industries or fields to solve our current problem?"
Result 2: Cross-pollination of ideas can inspire innovation. Look beyond your industry to identify successful strategies that can be adapted.

Question 3: "Are there emerging technologies or trends that could be leveraged to solve this problem more efficiently and effectively?"
Result 3: Stay updated on technology and trends. Consider how emerging tools or trends can be applied to your specific problem.

Question 4: "What if we approached this problem from the perspective of our customers or end-users? How might their insights lead to creative solutions?"

Result 4: Customer-centered thinking often sparks innovation. Involve end-users in the problem-solving process to gain valuable insights.

Question 5: "How can we create a culture that rewards and celebrates experimentation and risk-taking?"
Result 5: A culture that embraces experimentation encourages creativity. Recognize and celebrate employees who take calculated risks.

Question 6: "What opportunities exist for cross-functional collaboration and knowledge sharing within our team or organization?"
Result 6: Collaborative environments foster innovation. Explore ways to facilitate cross-functional collaboration and knowledge sharing.

Question 7: "How can we encourage continuous learning and skill development among team members to enhance their creativity and problem-solving abilities?"
Result 7: Invest in employee development. Provide opportunities for learning and skill development to fuel creativity.

Question 8: "What if we set aside dedicated time or resources for innovation projects and allowed team members to explore their passion projects?"
Result 8: Allocating time and resources for innovation projects can yield significant results. Allow team members to pursue their passion projects within the organization.

By incorporating these questions into your leadership strategy and actively engaging with your team to foster innovation and creativity, you can create an environment where new ideas are valued, and creative solutions are encouraged. This approach will position your team for success in an ever-evolving business landscape.

Series of Questions 2: Problem Solving and Decision-Making

Subcategory: Questions for Identifying Root Causes

Identifying the root causes of problems is essential for effective decision-making and problem-solving. Here are nine questions that will help you uncover underlying issues and make informed choices.

Question 1: "When did this problem first occur, and what were the initial signs or symptoms?"
Result 1: Understanding the problem's origin and early indicators provides valuable context for identifying root causes.

Question 2: "What factors or variables have changed since the problem's onset, and how might these changes be connected to its development?"
Result 2: Changes in variables can be crucial for identifying root causes. Analyze how alterations in factors may have contributed to the problem.

Question 3: "Have we encountered similar problems or challenges in the past? If so, what were the commonalities, and what can we learn from those experiences?"
Result 3: Past experiences offer insights. Recognizing patterns in previous challenges can lead to a better understanding of the current problem.

Question 4: "Who or what could be directly or indirectly linked to the problem? Are there stakeholders, processes, or external factors that warrant investigation?"

Result 4: Identifying connections and stakeholders is vital. Investigate all potential links to the problem, both internal and external.

Question 5: "What assumptions have we made about this problem, and how might these assumptions impact our understanding of its root causes?"

Result 5: Assumptions can cloud judgment. Evaluate the assumptions you've made and consider how they might influence your problem-solving approach.

Question 6: "Are there data or parameters available that can shed light on the problem? What do the data suggest about potential root causes?"

Result 6: Data can be a powerful tool. Analyze relevant data and use it to pinpoint potential root causes.

Question 7: "Have we sought input from all team members and relevant stakeholders? Are there perspectives we might have overlooked?"

Result 7: Comprehensive input is crucial. Ensure you've gathered insights from all relevant sources to avoid overlooking critical information.

Question 8: "What are the short-term and long-term consequences of the problem if left unresolved? How might these consequences guide our efforts to identify root causes?"

Result 8: Examining consequences provides motivation. Consider the impact of the problem over time to prioritize root cause identification.

Question 9: "What experiments or tests can we conduct to validate or refute potential root causes? How can we use the scientific method to guide our inquiry?"

Result 9: Scientific methods can be applied. Develop experiments or tests to systematically investigate and confirm or rule out potential root causes.

Using these questions in your decision-making and problem-solving processes will allow you to dig deeper, identify root causes more accurately, and make informed choices that address the core of complex issues. They provide a structured approach to uncovering underlying factors contributing to problems, enabling the development of effective solutions.

Subcategory: Questions for Generating Creative Solutions

Creativity is a valuable resource when it comes to problem-solving. These nine questions are designed to stimulate innovative ideas and guide you in finding creative solutions to complex challenges.

Question 1: "What unconventional approaches or out-of-the-box ideas can we explore to address this problem?"

Result 1: Embracing unconventional thinking can lead to groundbreaking solutions. Encourage brainstorming sessions to generate unique ideas.

Question 2: "How can we adapt successful strategies from other industries or fields to solve our current problem?"

Result 2: Cross-pollination of ideas can inspire innovation. Look beyond your industry to identify successful strategies that can be adapted.

Question 3: "Are there emerging technologies or trends that could be leveraged to solve this problem more efficiently and effectively?"

Result 3: Stay updated on technology and trends. Consider how emerging tools or trends could be applied to your specific problem.

Question 4: "What if we approached this problem from the perspective of our customers or end users? How might their insights lead to creative solutions?"

Result 4: Customer-centric thinking is valuable. Empathize with your customers and explore how their perspectives can inspire creative solutions.

Question 5: "Can we collaborate with external partners or experts specializing in areas related to our problem? How might their expertise contribute to creative solutions?"

Result 5: External collaboration can bring fresh insights. Seek out partners or experts who can provide unique perspectives.

Question 6: "What constraints or limitations can we remove or reframe to open up new possibilities for solving this problem?"

Result 6: Sometimes constraints stifle creativity. Identify and challenge constraints to explore previously unconsidered solutions.

Question 7: "How can we make the problem-solving process playful to engage our team and encourage innovative thinking?"

Result 7: Gamification can stimulate creativity. Turn the problem-solving process into a game to inspire enthusiasm and new ideas.

Question 8: "What analogies or metaphors can we draw upon to gain new insights into this problem?"
Result 8: Analogies can provide clarity. Use analogies or metaphors to explain the problem in different ways and gain new perspectives.

Question 9: "What if we were to flip our assumptions about this problem? How might this reversal lead to innovative solutions?"
Result 9: Flipping assumptions can spark creativity. Challenge conventional wisdom by considering the opposite approach.

Incorporating these questions into your problem-solving process can encourage creativity, foster innovative thinking, and explore a broader range of solutions to complex challenges. Embracing creativity allows you to discover new approaches that can lead to breakthroughs and positive outcomes.

Subcategory: Questions for Effective Decision-Making

Making informed and effective decisions is crucial in management and consulting. These nine questions are designed to guide you in the decision-making process and ensure that your choices align with your goals and values.

Question 1: "What is the primary objective or goal I intend to achieve with this decision?"
Result 1: Clarify your primary objective to ensure that your decision is focused and targeted. Define what success looks like.

Question 2: "Have I gathered all the relevant information and data needed to make an informed decision?"
Result 2: Research and collect information thoroughly to avoid making decisions based on assumptions or incomplete data.

Question 3: "What are the potential risks and benefits associated with each available option?"

Result 3: Evaluate the risks and benefits of each option to make a balanced decision. Consider short-term and long-term consequences.

Question 4: "How do my organization's values and principles align with each decision I'm considering?"

Result 4: Ensure that your decisions align with your organization's core values and principles to maintain consistency.

Question 5: "What are the ethical implications of each decision, and how do they align with my personal and professional ethics?"

Result 5: Consider the ethical dimensions of your decisions and make choices in line with your ethical framework.

Question 6: "Have I considered the potential impact of this decision on various stakeholders, including employees, customers, and shareholders?"

Result 6: Evaluate how your decision may affect different stakeholders and strive for outcomes that benefit all parties when possible.

Question 7: "Am I open to seeking input and feedback from others, and have I consulted with experts or colleagues?"

Result 7: Collaboration and consultation can lead to better decisions. Be open to others' suggestions and seek input from experts when necessary.

Question 8: "What is my timeline for making this decision, and how will I manage the implementation process?"

Result 8: Define a clear timeline for your decision-making process and consider how you will effectively implement your choice.

Question 9: "What contingency plans can I put in place to address potential challenges or unforeseen developments after making the decision?"
Result 9: Prepare for the unexpected by developing plans to address unforeseen challenges that may arise after the decision.

These questions provide a structured framework for effective decision-making. By carefully considering each aspect, you can make well-informed, ethical decisions that align with your goals and values. Effective decision-making is a fundamental skill for managers and consultants, and these questions will help you successfully address complex choices.

Questions series 3: Effective Communication and Conflict Resolution
Subcategory: Questions for Improving Communication

Effective communication is at the heart of successful management and consulting. These eight questions are designed to help you enhance your communication skills, build stronger relationships, and resolve conflicts more efficiently.

Question 1: "Am I actively listening to understand, or am I listening to respond?"
Result 1: Actively listen by giving your full attention to the speaker, seeking to understand their point of view before formulating your response.

Question 2: "What non-verbal signals am I conveying, and how might they be interpreted by others?"
Result 2: Be aware of your body language, facial expressions, and tone of voice, as they can significantly impact how your message is received.

Question 3: "Am I asking open-ended questions that encourage meaningful conversations?"
Result 3: Use open-ended questions to promote deeper discussions and gather more comprehensive information.

Question 4: "Am I providing constructive feedback rather than criticism or blame?"
Result 4: Offer feedback focused on improvement and solutions rather than assigning blame or criticism.

Question 5: "Do I understand and respect the cultural and personal differences of those I'm communicating with?"
Result 5: Recognize and appreciate the diversity of perspectives and backgrounds in your communication, promoting an inclusive environment.

Question 6: "Have I proactively addressed potential misunderstandings or misinterpretations?"
Result 6: Clarify any misunderstandings immediately to prevent conflicts or communication issues from escalating.

Question 7: "Am I practicing empathy by considering the emotions and perspectives of others?"
Result 7: Empathize with others by understanding their feelings and viewpoints, even if you don't agree with them.

Question 8: "Have I explored mutually beneficial solutions during conflicts, aiming for outcomes that benefit all parties?"

Result 8: Seek win-win solutions in conflicts by finding common ground and options that benefit all involved parties.

These questions serve as valuable tools for improving your communication skills and resolving conflicts more effectively. By incorporating these practices into your professional interactions, you can build stronger relationships, promote collaboration, and create a positive work environment in both managerial and consulting roles. Effective communication is the cornerstone of success in any field, and these questions will help you excel in this critical area.

Subcategory: Questions for Navigating and Resolving Conflicts

Conflict is an inevitable part of any workplace, but how you handle it can make a significant difference. These eight questions are designed to guide you in navigating and resolving conflicts constructively.

Question 1: "What is the root cause of this conflict, and how can we address it?"
Result 1: Identifying underlying issues is essential for resolving conflicts. Once the root cause is identified, we can work on a solution to address it.

Question 2: "Are all parties involved in the conflict aware of each other's perspectives and concerns?"
Result 2: Ensuring that all involved parties understand each other's viewpoints can lead to better empathy and more effective conflict resolution.

Question 3: "Have we established basic rules and a respectful communication process for addressing conflicts?"

Result 3: Creating a framework for addressing conflicts, such as basic rules and guidelines for respectful communication, can help manage conflicts more productively.

Question 4: "What are the potential consequences of not resolving this conflict promptly and effectively?"
Result 4: Understanding the potential negative outcomes of unresolved conflicts can provide motivation to address and resolve them.

Question 5: "Are there compromises or concessions that can be made to find a mutually beneficial solution?"
Result 5: In many conflicts, finding middle ground and compromises can lead to solutions that benefit all parties involved.

Question 6: "Have we considered involving a neutral third party or mediator if the conflict remains unresolved?"
Result 6: Sometimes, involving an impartial mediator can help facilitate more productive discussions and resolutions.

Question 7: "How can we ensure that the resolution of this conflict leads to improved communication and collaboration in the future?"
Result 7: It's essential to focus on long-term solutions that enhance working relationships and prevent similar conflicts in the future.

Question 8: "Have we documented the resolution and any actions taken to hold all parties accountable?"
Result 8: Documenting the resolution and action steps helps ensure that everyone remains accountable and follows through on commitments.

These questions are valuable tools for managing and resolving conflicts in a professional context. By addressing conflicts constructively and focusing on finding solutions, you can promote a positive and collaborative work environment. Effective conflict resolution is a vital skill for managers and consultants, and these questions will guide you toward positive outcomes.

Subcategory: Questions for Improving Team Dynamics

Effective teamwork is the cornerstone of a successful organization. Use these eight questions to enhance team dynamics and promote a collaborative and harmonious work environment.

Question 1: "What are the unique strengths and weaknesses of each team member, and how can we leverage them effectively?"
Result 1: Understanding individual strengths and weaknesses allows us to assign tasks in line with each team member's abilities, promoting success.

Question 2: "Are our team's purposes and goals clear to everyone and aligned with the organization's mission?"
Result 2: Ensuring that all team members understand their roles and how they contribute to the broader mission of the organization promotes focus and cohesion.

Question 3: "How can we encourage open and honest communication within the team?"
Result 3: Open communication is essential for resolving conflicts and promoting collaboration. Encourage team members to freely share ideas and concerns.

Question 4: "What strategies can we implement to celebrate the team's achievements and build a sense of unity?"
Result 4: Recognizing and celebrating the team's successes creates a positive atmosphere and strengthens a sense of belonging.

Question 5: "Have we established a process for providing constructive feedback and performance evaluations?"
Result 5: Regular feedback sessions help team members understand their strengths and areas for improvement, contributing to professional growth.

Question 6: "Are there opportunities for team-building activities outside of work to strengthen personal relationships?"
Result 6: Team-building activities can foster camaraderie and improve collaboration by allowing team members to connect on a personal level.

Question 7: "What measures can we take to ensure that all team members feel valued and included?"
Result 7: Inclusion is vital for team dynamics. Implement practices that make every team member feel valued and heard.

Question 8: "How can we adapt our team dynamics to changing circumstances or challenges?"
Result 8: Being flexible and adaptable as a team ensures effective response to new challenges and resilience.

These questions are valuable tools for improving team dynamics within your organization. By promoting open communication, recognizing individual strengths, and fostering a sense of unity, you can create a team that is not only more productive but also more resilient in the face of challenges. Effective team dynamics are crucial for success in both managerial and consulting roles, and these questions will guide you in achieving just that.

Series of Questions 4: Change Management and Strategic Development

Subcategory: Questions for Organizational Change Management

Change is a constant in the business world. These eight questions will help you successfully navigate organizational change and ensure that your strategies align with evolving goals.

Question 1: "What is the driving force behind the need for change within our organization?"
Result 1: Understanding the catalyst for change provides valuable context and helps articulate the need for change to stakeholders.

Question 2: "Who are the key stakeholders affected by this change, and how can we involve them in the process?"
Result 2: Involving key stakeholders fosters a sense of ownership and ensures their insights are considered during the change process.

Question 3: "What potential challenges or resistance might we encounter during the change process, and how can we proactively address them?"
Result 3: Identifying potential obstacles allows for the creation of mitigation strategies, reducing resistance to change.

Question 4: "What impact will this change have on our organizational culture, and how can we align it with our strategic goals?"

Result 4: Ensuring that change aligns with the desired organizational culture is crucial for long-term success.

Question 5: "What communication strategies can we implement to keep all employees informed and engaged during the change?"
Result 5: Clear and consistent communication helps employees understand the purpose of the change and their role in its success.

Question 6: "What resources, training, or support will be needed to help employees adapt to the change?"
Result 6: Providing the necessary resources and training ensures that employees have the tools they need to succeed in the new environment.

Question 7: "How will we measure the effectiveness of this change, and what key performance indicators (KPIs) should we monitor?"
Result 7: Defining KPIs allows for the assessment of the change's impact and necessary adjustments based on data.

Question 8: "What strategies can we use to support the positive aspects of this change in the long term?"
Result 8: Sustainability is essential. Identifying strategies to maintain positive changes ensures lasting benefits.

These questions will guide you in effectively managing organizational change. By considering driving forces, involving stakeholders, proactively addressing challenges, and focusing on sustainability, you can approach change with confidence and align it with your organization's strategic goals. Change management is a crucial aspect of leadership and consulting, and these questions will help you excel in this vital role.

Subcategory: Questions for Strategic Planning and Execution

Strategic planning and execution are at the heart of organizational success. These nine questions will guide you in developing and implementing strategies that drive positive change and achieve your long-term goals.

Question 1: "What are the long-term goals of our organization, and how do they align with our mission and vision?"
Result 1: Aligning long-term goals with your mission and vision ensures that your strategies are purpose-driven.

Question 2: "Who are our key stakeholders, and what are their expectations for the future of our organization?"
Result 2: Understanding stakeholder expectations allows you to tailor your strategies to meet their needs.

Question 3: "What are the current market trends and industry challenges that may impact our strategic planning?"
Result 3: Staying informed about market trends and challenges ensures that your strategies remain adaptable and relevant.

Question 4: "How can we leverage our organization's strengths to seize opportunities and overcome weaknesses?"
Result 4: Identifying strengths and weaknesses helps develop strategies that capitalize on advantages.

Question 5: "What specific actions and initiatives are needed to achieve our strategic goals, and what is the timeline for their implementation?"
Result 5: Creating a detailed action plan with deadlines ensures that your strategies are actionable and achievable.

Question 6: "Who are the individuals or teams responsible for executing each aspect of our strategic plan?"
Result 6: Assigning clear responsibilities ensures accountability and effective execution.

Question 7: "How will we measure progress and success in our strategic initiatives, and what key performance indicators (KPIs) should we monitor?"
Result 7: Defining KPIs allows for progress tracking and data-driven decision-making.

Question 8: "What potential risks or obstacles might we encounter during the execution of our strategic plan, and how can we mitigate them?"
Result 8: Identifying risks and mitigation strategies promotes smoother execution.

Question 9: "How will we ensure that our long-term strategies remain aligned with our organization's mission and values as we evolve?"
Result 9: Regularly revisiting your mission and values helps maintain alignment with your long-term vision.

These questions provide a solid framework for strategic planning and execution. By defining success, addressing cultural changes, engaging employees, ensuring necessary resources, and proactively managing challenges, you can develop and execute strategies that drive positive change and steer your organization toward long-term success. Strategic planning and execution are essential skills for managers and consultants, and these questions will help you excel in these roles.

Subcategory: Questions for Long-Term Success

Achieving long-term success requires a strategic approach to change management. These nine questions will guide you in planning for sustainability and growth in a dynamic business environment.

Question 1: "How do we define long-term success for our organization, and what are the key milestones along the way?"
Result 1: Defining success and setting milestones provides a clear roadmap for your organization's journey.

Question 2: "What cultural changes, if any, are necessary to support our long-term goals and strategic initiatives?"
Result 2: Aligning organizational culture with long-term goals ensures lasting progress.

Question 3: "How can we engage employees at all levels to become champions of change and contribute to long-term success?"
Result 3: Engaged employees play a critical role in driving long-term success; involve them in the change process.

Question 4: "What resources, including talent and technology, are required to support our long-term strategic initiatives?"
Result 4: Identifying necessary resources ensures that your organization is well-equipped for the journey ahead.

Question 5: "What potential obstacles or resistance might we encounter during the implementation of long-term strategies, and how can we address them effectively?"
Result 5: Addressing challenges and resistance in advance facilitates smoother implementation.

Question 6: "How can we maintain flexibility and adaptability in our long-term plans to respond to evolving market conditions?"

Result 6: Long-term success requires the ability to pivot and adapt as needed.

Question 7: "What role does innovation play in sustaining our long-term competitive advantage, and how can we promote an innovation culture?"

Result 7: Innovation is essential for staying relevant and competitive; encourage a culture that values innovation.

Question 8: "What parameters and key performance indicators (KPIs) will we use to measure progress toward long-term success?"

Result 8: Clearly defined metrics provide a basis for assessing progress and making informed decisions.

Question 9: "How will we ensure that our long-term strategies remain aligned with the mission and values of our organization as we evolve?"

Result 9: Regularly revisiting your mission and values helps maintain alignment with your long-term vision.

These questions offer a robust framework for change management and long-term success. By defining success, addressing cultural shifts, engaging employees, securing necessary resources, and proactively managing challenges, you can set your organization on a path toward sustainable growth and success. Change management and long-term strategic planning are essential skills for managers and consultants, and these questions will help you excel in these roles.

Chapter 9: Case Studies and Real-Life Examples

Case Study 1: Transforming a Struggling Team Through Systemic Leadership

Introduction: Setting the Scene:

In the annals of management, the story of Sarah Mitchell stands as a beacon of inspiration, a testament to the transformative power of systemic leadership, and the profound impact that arises from asking the right systemic questions.

Imagine this: Sarah stepping into her role as the manager of a beleaguered software development team at Tech Innovators Inc. The challenges she faced were formidable, and the odds seemed stacked against her. The team, once a center of innovation, had plunged into a state of chronic underperformance. Missed deadlines, high turnover, and low morale had become the unfortunate norm. The ghosts of the previous autocratic regime loomed large, leaving the team disheartened, disengaged, and demotivated.

But Sarah was no ordinary manager. She possessed a secret weapon: the art of systemic leadership and the ability to ask the right systemic questions. It was a journey to rekindle hope, foster trust, and ignite the flames of productivity.

The Challenges? They were the crucible in which Sarah's leadership would be forged.

1. Low morale and trust: The team's trust in leadership had eroded, and morale had plummeted under the weight of constant pressure and micromanagement.
2. Disrupted communication: Effective communication was a distant memory among team members, leaving behind a trail of misunderstandings and conflicts.
3. Missed deadlines: The constant stream of project delays had tarnished the company's reputation, and customer satisfaction was at an all-time low.

The Approach of Systemic Questions:

What sets Sarah apart is the awareness that a systemic approach is the key to unraveling the tangled threads of her team's challenges. She embarked on her transformation journey by asking a series of systemic questions, each of which served as a compass guiding her through the labyrinth of complexity:

- What is the root cause of low morale and low trust within the team?

This question took her to the heart of the matter, uncovering deep-seated issues that had been festering for too long.

- How can I create an environment where team members feel valued and heard?

With this question, she laid the foundation for a culture of respect and open dialogue, where every voice mattered.

- What changes are needed in our communication processes to improve collaboration?

This question opened the doors to effective communication, dispelling the misunderstandings that had plagued the team.

- How can we regain our reputation for meeting project deadlines?

Sarah tackled this challenge head-on, aligning her team's efforts with a renewed commitment to excellence.

Sarah's journey was not just about managing a team; it was about guiding the team toward a better future. Her systemic leadership and the art of asking the right systemic questions breathed new life into her team. Morale skyrocketed, trust was rekindled, and the specter of missed deadlines faded into oblivion.

Sarah's story is a testament to the incredible potential that lies within a leader armed with systemic questions. It reminds us that challenges are not obstacles but springboards to greatness. In every organization, there's a Sarah waiting to emerge, armed with questions that have the power to transform. Will you be the one to ask?

Implementation:

Sarah Mitchell's journey is a testament to the transformative power of leadership guided by asking the right questions. It's a story that inspires us to see challenges not as insurmountable obstacles but as opportunities for growth and innovation.

Sarah knew that trust was the foundation of any high-performing team. She didn't just hope for trust to magically appear; she took courageous action. She orchestrated a team-building retreat, a safe space where team members could share their fears, hopes, and expectations. Through the magic of systemic questions, she created an environment where candid conversations thrived. Questions like "What can we do to improve trust among team members?" and "What changes can we make to enhance collaboration?" were her favorite tools. With these questions, she dismantled the walls of distrust one brick at a time, revealing a foundation of trust underneath.

The next chapter of Sarah's journey was dedicated to revitalizing communication, the lifeblood of success. She knew that simply talking wasn't enough; it had to be targeted and effective communication. Sarah transformed the team's regular meetings into arenas for constructive feedback and collaborative problem-solving. Armed with systemic questions, she painted a canvas of effective communication. She asked, "How can we improve our communication processes?" inviting team members to share their insights. She inquired, "What barriers hinder effective collaboration?" uncovering layers of communication issues. In this space, the team's voice grew louder, concerns found their audience, and solutions harmonized.

However, Sarah's quest was not complete. The specter of missed deadlines haunted her team. She tackled this challenge by systematically identifying bottlenecks and challenges in project management. Systemic questions became their guiding stars. "What are the major obstacles to meeting project deadlines?" she asked, encouraging the team to unveil the issues. "How can we streamline our project management processes?" she prompted, guiding them toward efficient workflows and better time management. With these illuminating questions lighting their path, the team embarked on a journey of discovery, uncovering gems of efficiency that had eluded them.

Sarah's leadership journey is a masterpiece. Through systemic questions, she revived trust, reignited communication, and defeated the specter of missed deadlines. Her story reminds us that leadership isn't about having all the answers; it's about asking the right questions and giving others the opportunity to do the same. It invites all leaders to take a page from Sarah's book and embark on their own journey of transformation, one question at a time.

Results:

Over time, Sarah's systemic leadership approach began to yield remarkable results:

1. Improved morale: Team members reported feeling more valued and engaged. Morale significantly improved as trust was rebuilt.
2. Effective communication: Team communication became more transparent and collaborative. Misunderstandings decreased, and conflicts were resolved more constructively.
3. Meeting deadlines: Projects were completed on time, resulting in increased customer satisfaction and a regained reputation for reliability.

Key Takeaways:

This case study highlights the transformative power of systemic questions when navigating the labyrinth of multi-faceted crises. Within its pages, key lessons emerge as beacons:

- Root Cause Analysis: To find lasting solutions, you must embark on a quest to identify and address the root causes of the problem.
- Stakeholder Engagement: Involving stakeholders in a harmonious dialogue guided by systemic questions paves the way for well-informed decisions and resolutions.
- Transparency and Communication: In the grand tapestry of rebuilding trust, the threads of open,

honest, and empathetic communication are woven
with threads of gold.

- Strategic Decision-Making: When navigating stormy
  waters, systemic questions must be the guiding stars in
  the realm of strategic decision-making.

The triumph of crisis resolution by GlobalTech Inc. is a
resounding anthem to the ability to challenge the system
even in the most turbulent circumstances. As you embark on
your odyssey through the following chapters, the brilliance of
these principles will be revealed in all their splendor. Let them
be your guiding constellations in the vast cosmos of
managerial and consultancy roles, for they will illuminate your
path to enduring success.

Case Study 2: Resolving a Complex Organizational Crisis with Systemic Questions

Introduction: An Ongoing Crisis:

Embark on a journey through this enlightening case study, a
testament to the resilience of a multinational corporation,
GlobalTech Inc. Here, we discover the gripping narrative of a
company grappling with a multifaceted crisis that threatened
not only its reputation but also its very financial foundation.
Prepare to witness an extraordinary transformation where the
power of systemic questions and strategic decision-making
takes center stage, guiding GlobalTech Inc. to a triumphant
resolution of this intricate challenge.

The Background:

In the annals of the technology sector, GlobalTech Inc. stood as an emblem of innovation and global prowess. Yet, a crisis storm raged over this titan:

1. The shadow of doubt: A major product recall loomed, driven by potential safety issues, casting a dark financial cloud.
2. The roar of discontent: Labor disputes erupted, manifesting as strikes in crucial production facilities, testing the company's resolve.
3. A media tempest: Negative media coverage and an unrelenting wave of social media backlash surged, tarnishing the once-pristine reputation of the company.
4. A stock market saga: The crisis unleashed a financial whirlwind, causing the company's stock price to plummet—a daunting call to arms for both shareholders and investors.

The Approach of Systemic Questions

In the eye of the hurricane, GlobalTech's CEO, the visionary David Reynolds, remained unwavering. He recognized that traditional problem-solving tools would be insufficient for this Herculean task. Thus, he turned to a systemic approach of asking questions, a beacon of hope to navigate the labyrinthine crisis.

With unwavering determination, David posed crucial questions, each of which was a beam of light piercing the darkness:

*   What seeds gave rise to this intricate crisis?
*   How can we bridge the gap between employee concerns and customer expectations?

- What complex steps must we take to rebuild public trust and resurrect our tarnished reputation?

Prepare to be inspired as we journey through the saga of GlobalTech. It's a story that highlights the transformative power of leadership guided by asking the right questions, where resilience and innovation emerge victorious against the darkest odds. The message is clear: embrace the art of systemic questions, and you too can conquer complexity, emerging stronger, wiser, and victorious.

Implementation:

Identifying Root Causes: When the storm raged, GlobalTech formed an elite crisis management team, a beacon of hope drawn from the realms of various departments. These intrepid experts wielded systemic questions as their mighty swords, tearing aside the veil to reveal the root causes. They asked, "What unfurled the flag of product safety issues?" and "Why did labor disputes fan their burning embers?" These questions were the torches illuminating the darkest corners.

Stakeholder Engagement: A realization emerged: stakeholders held the key. The team embarked on a journey to engage with them, armed with systemic questions as their compass. To unravel the tangled threads of employee concerns and customer expectations, they asked, "What remedies can soothe employee grievances?" and "What bridges can we build to restore trust among our customers?" These questions opened the doors to understanding.

Strategic Decision-Making: Systemic questions guided the helm of strategic decisions. The team navigated through stormy seas, asking, "How can we reshape our production processes to ensure product safety?" and "What safeguards can we build to increase employee satisfaction and quell the storm of strikes?" With these questions, they charted a course to safer shores.

Communication Strategy: A symphony of communication was composed, notes of transparency and empathy interweaving in every chord. The crisis team held systemic questions high, like guiding stars. They asked, "How can we etch our commitment to safety in the annals of customer trust?" and "What melodies will resonate with our employees?" These questions were the orchestrators of harmony.

Results:

And lo, the fruits of their courage blossomed:

1. Crisis resolution: Product safety issues were overcome, and production processes were reborn, heralding a triumphant product relaunch.
2. Labor dispute resolution: By embracing employees and listening to their grievances, strikes subsided, and labor relations saw a new dawn.
3. Reputation restoration: Transparency and keeping promises rebuilt the castle of public trust, adorning the company's reputation with splendor.
4. Stock price recovery: As the crisis abated, the company's stock price soared, reigniting the confidence of both shareholders and investors.

Bear witness to the story of GlobalTech, where systemic questions and strategic decision-making could cast a radiant light on a path strewn with darkness. This story reminds us that through resilience, innovation, and the right questions, even the most violent storms can be tamed, and a brighter horizon awaits. Let it be a guiding beacon for all those seeking to harness the power of systemic questions in their own journey of transformation and triumph.

Key Takeaways:

This case study highlights the extraordinary potential of systemic questions when navigating the labyrinth of multi-faceted crises. Within its pages, key lessons stand as beacons:

- Root Cause Analysis: To find lasting solutions, you must embark on a quest to identify and address the root causes of the problem.
- Stakeholder Engagement: Involving stakeholders in a harmonious dialogue guided by systemic questions paves the way for well-informed decisions and resolutions.
- Transparency and Communication: In the grand tapestry of rebuilding trust, the threads of open, honest, and empathetic communication are woven with threads of gold.
- Strategic Decision-Making: When navigating stormy waters, systemic questions must be the guiding stars in the realm of strategic decision-making.

The triumph of crisis resolution by GlobalTech Inc. is a resounding anthem to the ability to challenge the system even in the most turbulent circumstances. As you embark on your odyssey through the following chapters, the brilliance of these principles will be revealed in all their splendor. Let them be your guiding constellations in the vast cosmos of managerial and consultancy roles, for they will illuminate your path to enduring success.

Case Study 3: Implementing Strategic Changes with Systemic Consulting

Introduction: The Challenge of Organizational Transformation:

In this captivating case study, we invite you to embark on a journey alongside Midland Financial Services, a medium-sized financial institution navigating the winds of change in a rapidly evolving industry. Prepare to witness the profound impact of systemic consulting, where the guiding light of systemic questions orchestrated strategic metamorphoses that breathed new life into the organization.

1. Setting the Stage: Midland Financial Services, once a regional titan in the financial sector, faced a series of formidable challenges that threatened its legacy:
2. Market Disruption: The financial sector, swept by the winds of fintech startups and shifting customer preferences, stood on the brink of transformation.
3. Declining Profitability: The company's profitability, once a beacon, had diminished due to outdated processes and a lack of innovation.
4. Employee Disengagement: The lifeblood of the company, its employees, saw their morale plummet, casting shadows of reduced productivity and high turnover.
5. Stagnant Growth: Once-vibrant growth at Midland Financial had given way to stagnation, issuing a clear call for radical reinvention.

The Approach of Systemic Consulting:

Midland Financial's CEO, the visionary Sarah Anderson, recognized the need for a comprehensive approach to ignite transformation. Embracing systemic consulting, a framework steeped in the wisdom of understanding interconnection, became the catalyst for change. This odyssey began with a symphony of systemic questions:

- What systemic forces weave the tapestry of declining profitability and stagnation?
- How can we empower and encourage our employees to steer the ship of innovation and navigate the seas of change?
- What strategic constellations must we follow to reposition Midland Financial as the North Star in a rapidly evolving cosmos?

Prepare to be inspired as we unveil the chapters that tell this epic story of reinvention. The saga of Midland Financial Services serves as a testament to the boundless potential of systemic questions and consulting in reshaping destinies. Join us, for within these chapters lies the blueprint for your transformative odyssey in the realm of change and organizational progress.

Implementation:

Understanding Systemic Factors: The consulting team embarked on a journey of discovery, delving into the inner workings of Midland Financial Services. At every level, employees were invited to the table, their voices a chorus of wisdom in uncovering the systemic factors that had woven the tapestry of challenges. Questions like, "Which internal processes hinder our adaptability?" and "How does our organizational culture impact employee engagement?" were the compass guiding this profound introspection.

Employee Empowerment: At the heart of this transformation was a profound realization: empowered employees hold the keys to innovation and resilience. The consulting team, guided by systemic questions, sought ways to instill this power. "What initiatives would make employees feel more involved in the decision-making process?" and "How can we create a culture of continuous learning?" breathed life into this transformation, shaping a culture where every employee was a guardian of change.

Strategic Changes: A strategic metamorphosis was enticing, and systemic questions were the architects of this revolution. "What strategic changes can position us as leaders in this evolving industry?" and "How can we leverage technology to enhance our services?" paved the way to a reinvented future, where Midland Financial would shine once again as the North Star.

Change Management: Change, while essential, often reveals uncertainty. Focusing on the human side of change, implementation unfolded gradually, and systemic questions stood guard over adaptability. Concerns were addressed with empathy, and solutions evolved. Each step was a testament to the resilience of the human spirit.

Results:

The crescendo of this journey is marked by achievements:

1. Restored Profitability: The organization's profitability, like a phoenix, began its ascent as outdated processes crumbled, and cost efficiency soared.
2. Culture of Innovation: At the heart of Midland Financial, a culture centered on innovation was nurtured, fueled by engaged employees who felt valued and encouraged to contribute their ideas.

3. Growth Revival: Dormant seeds of growth sprouted once again as Midland Financial danced to the ever-evolving rhythms of customer needs and preferences.
4. Employee Engagement: The melody of employee engagement reached new heights, resulting in increased productivity and the end of the turnover storm.

Key Points:

This case study highlights the potential of systemic consulting, unveiling guiding principles:

- Systemic Analysis: A deep understanding of systemic factors is the cornerstone of change.
- Employee Empowerment: Empowerment and employee engagement are the sparks of innovation and adaptation.
- Strategic Agility: Adaptability is the compass guiding organizations through the labyrinth of change.
- Change Management: Change must be embraced with empathy, and adaptability is the key to a harmonious transformation.

Midland Financial Services, once adrift in turbulent waters, stands as a testament to the transformative power of systemic consulting. The art of asking systemic questions guided this journey, and its echoes beckon you. As you journey through these chapters, let the symphony of transformation inspire your managerial and consulting endeavors. In the realm of organizational change, your potential knows no bounds.

Case Study 4: Creating a Successful Corporate Culture with Systemic Leadership

Introduction: The Challenge of Corporate Culture

Settle in for this fascinating case study that will take us inside BrightHorizon Enterprises, a company with a history of steady growth but a corporate culture in need of critical evolution. This is the tale of how systemic leadership and the art of asking the right systemic questions played a pivotal role in shaping a culture of success.

Background:

BrightHorizon Enterprises, a company in the technology sector, had reached a turning point. As global interest in environmental issues grew, there was increasing pressure to expand and capitalize on this opportunity. However, the company had a history of unsustainable business practices, making it challenging to pivot in this new direction.

The Approach of Systemic Questions:

BrightHorizon's CEO, Alex Turner, realized that achieving sustainable growth required a holistic approach. He began asking a series of key systemic questions to guide the growth strategy:

- What unsustainable business practices are hindering our growth?
- How can we develop a growth strategy that aligns with environmental principles?
- What are the key sustainability metrics we should monitor to ensure our environmental responsibility?

Implementation:

The transformation of BrightHorizon took shape through these key steps guided by systemic questions:

- Reviewing Business Practices: Alex conducted a comprehensive review of company practices, identifying areas where improvements were needed. He asked, "Which unsustainable business practices should we eliminate or replace?" This question led to significant changes in company operations.
- Developing a Sustainable Growth Strategy: Alex worked with the leadership team to create a growth strategy based on sustainability principles. He asked, "How can we expand in a way that is in harmony with the environment?" This question led to the diversification of the company's offerings toward more eco-friendly solutions.
- Monitoring Sustainability: Alex introduced a performance monitoring system for environmental metrics and asked, "What are the key sustainability measures we should monitor to ensure our environmental responsibility?" This question helped hold the company accountable for its actions.

Results:

BrightHorizon experienced sustainable growth:

1. Improved Business Practices: The company eliminated unsustainable practices, reducing its environmental impact.
2. Sustainable Growth Strategy: BrightHorizon expanded by offering innovative environmental solutions, gaining the trust of environmentally-conscious customers.

3. Sustainability Monitoring: The company was able to demonstrate its commitment to the environment through transparent sustainability data and measures.

This case study demonstrates how systemic questions can play a key role in shaping a sustainable growth strategy. Through holistic assessment and a realignment of business practices, BrightHorizon Enterprises emerged stronger than ever.

Case Study 5: Implementing a Sustainable Growth Strategy through Systemic Questions

Introduction: The Challenge of Sustainable Growth

In this fascinating case study, we'll dive into the story of GreenSolutions, an environmental company with an ambitious goal: to grow sustainably. We'll discover how systemic questions played a crucial role in shaping a sustainable growth strategy and guiding the company to success.

Background:

GreenSolutions, a company dedicated to providing innovative environmental solutions, reached a turning point. As global interest in environmental sustainability grew, there was increasing pressure to expand and capitalize on this opportunity. However, the company had a history of unsustainable business practices, making it challenging to adapt to this new direction.

The Approach of Systemic Questions:

GreenSolutions' CEO, Emily Patterson, realized that achieving sustainable growth required a holistic approach. She began asking a series of key systemic questions to guide the growth strategy:

- What unsustainable business practices are hindering our growth?
- How can we develop a growth strategy that aligns with environmental principles?
- What are the key sustainability metrics we should monitor to ensure our environmental responsibility?

Implementation:

The transformation of GreenSolutions took shape through these key steps guided by systemic questions:

- Reviewing Business Practices: Emily conducted a comprehensive review of company practices, identifying areas where improvements were needed. She asked, "Which unsustainable business practices should we eliminate or replace?" This question led to significant changes in company operations.
- Developing a Sustainable Growth Strategy: Emily worked with the leadership team to create a growth strategy based on sustainability principles. She asked, "How can we expand in a way that is in harmony with the environment?" This question led to the diversification of the company's offerings toward more eco-friendly solutions.
- Monitoring Sustainability: Emily introduced a performance monitoring system for environmental metrics and asked, "What are the key sustainability measures we should monitor to ensure our

environmental responsibility?" This question helped hold the company accountable for its actions.

Results:

GreenSolutions experienced sustainable growth:

1. Improved Business Practices: The company eliminated unsustainable practices, reducing its environmental impact.
2. Sustainable Growth Strategy: GreenSolutions expanded by offering innovative environmental solutions, gaining the trust of environmentally-conscious customers.
3. Sustainability Monitoring: The company was able to demonstrate its commitment to the environment through transparent sustainability data and measures.

This case study demonstrates how systemic questions can play a key role in shaping a sustainable growth strategy. Through holistic assessment and a realignment of business practices, GreenSolutions became a leader in the environmental sector.

Chapter 10: Developing Skills in Systemic Questions

Tools and Techniques to Improve the Ability to Ask Systemic Questions

A key tool for improving the ability to ask systemic questions is practice. Like any skill, the more you practice, the better you become. In the realm of systemic questions, this means practicing observing situations, identifying hidden connections, and formulating relevant questions. Practice will help you develop a deeper intuition for how to effectively apply this approach. Another important technique is active listening. To ask effective systemic questions, you must first fully understand the situation. This requires attentive and unbiased listening, where you are open to different perspectives and capable of grasping details and nuances. Active listening will provide you with the necessary information to formulate relevant questions. A third fundamental tool is the ability to see the big picture. Systemic questions require a broad view and the ability to connect the parts to a whole system. Learning to recognize patterns, interactions, and relationships among different elements is crucial for asking questions that positively influence the situation. Furthermore, the practice of open-ended questions is essential. Questions that begin with "how," "why," "what," and "in what way" encourage people to reflect and explore further. These questions open the doors to discussion and the discovery of valuable information. Feedback is also a powerful learning tool. Ask colleagues, mentors, or coaches to assess your skills in the art of asking systemic questions. Feedback will help you identify areas for improvement and refine your skills over time. Throughout this chapter, we will explore these techniques in detail, providing practical examples and training scenarios to help you develop and refine your skills in the art of systemic questions. Mastery of these skills will allow you to successfully apply the systemic approach to management, consulting, coaching, and leadership, contributing to your own success and the success of the organizations you work with.

Practical Exercises and Training Activities

Another key element in developing your skills in systemic questions is the use of practical exercises and training activities. These active learning methods allow you to put into practice what you have learned and refine your skills in a controlled context. Practical exercises are an effective way to gain direct experience in applying systemic questions. You can start with relatively simple practice situations and gradually advance to more complex scenarios. For example, you could begin with coaching or consulting exercises where you practice the art of asking systemic questions about simulated cases. This will allow you to gain confidence and experience different strategies and approaches. Training activities are another valuable tool for developing skills in systemic questions. Participating in workshops, courses, or specific training sessions on this topic will give you the opportunity to learn from others' experiences, engage with experienced professionals, and gain new perspectives. Experienced instructors can guide you through practical exercises, discuss real cases, and share their in-depth knowledge.

It is important to emphasize that learning systemic questions is an ongoing process. The more practice and training you receive, the more competent you become. Additionally, the constant use of systemic questions in your daily professional practice is essential to maintain and improve your skills over time. Consider the opportunity to form or lead study or practice groups with colleagues or coaches interested in the same topic. These interactions can promote discussion, knowledge sharing, and collaborative learning, which can lead to significant growth in your skills in systemic questions. These experiences will help you become a more effective professional in coaching, consulting, leadership, and management, allowing you to address organizational challenges more consciously and competently.

Improving Your Systemic Thinking Skills

A crucial aspect of developing skills in systemic questions is improving your systemic thinking ability. This is a fundamental element in becoming an effective professional in applying systemic questions in various contexts, including coaching, consulting, leadership, and management. Systemic thinking is the ability to consider and understand the relationships and interconnections among different parts of a system or organization. This type of thinking goes beyond surface analysis and linear reasoning. Instead, it requires a broader view and the ability to identify the complex dynamics that influence the functioning of a system.

To improve your systemic thinking ability, it is important to adopt some key practices:

- **Careful Observation**: Dedicate time to careful observation of the organization or system you are examining. Take note of the relationships, patterns, and interactions that emerge. This will help you develop a deeper understanding of the dynamics involved.

- **Analysis of Interconnections**: Try to identify how different parts of the system influence each other. For example, how can decisions made in one department impact another? How can changes in one sector propagate to other sectors?
- **Long-Term Thinking**: Consider the long-term implications of actions and decisions. How might they influence the future of the organization? This type of perspective will help you avoid short-term solutions that could create problems in the long run.
- **Feedback Analysis**: Examine feedback and feedback loops within the system. How is information and data exchanged and used within the organization? Feedback can reveal hidden dynamics and provide valuable information for improvement.
- **Continuous Learning**: Systemic thinking is a skill that develops over time. Seek learning opportunities and knowledge acquisition to broaden your perspective and improve your systemic thinking ability.
- **Practice of Systemic Questions**: Actively use systemic questions in analyzing and assessing systems or organizations. This will help you put systemic thinking into concrete practice.

Additionally, consider collaborating with other professionals who have experience in systemic thinking. Engaging with different perspectives can enrich your understanding and lead to new ideas and solutions. Improving your systemic thinking ability is essential to becoming an expert in the use of systemic questions. This type of thinking will allow you to analyze, understand, and effectively influence systems and organizations, leading to significant and sustainable results in your coaching, consulting, leadership, and management activities.

Conclusion

Summary of Key Concepts

In conclusion, this book has been a journey through the powerful world of systemic questions and systemic thinking, a journey that has revealed a treasure trove of tools and approaches for managers, coaches, and consultants committed to leading and improving their organizations. We have explored how systemic questions represent a revolutionary perspective in problem-solving and organizational dynamics management. They have taught us to consider our professional world as an interconnected fabric, where every action has an impact, and every element is linked to others. We have discussed circular thinking, which has pushed us to look beyond linear cause-and-effect relationships, opening the door to a deeper understanding of the cyclical interactions that drive organizational dynamics. This has helped us uncover hidden dynamics and avoid superficial solutions.

Systemic questions have also taught us to look beyond the obvious symptoms, exploring the roots of problems. This broad-spectrum perspective has allowed us to avoid palliative solutions and address the true causes of organizational challenges. We have learned to identify the potential chain reaction of actions, recognizing that causes can become effects and vice versa. This has provided us with a valuable tool for managing change effectively.

The book has also urged us to look objectively, setting aside biases and personal interpretations to observe facts and dynamics with fresh eyes. This clarity of vision has been crucial in identifying the real challenges and opportunities within organizations. Furthermore, this guide for managers dealing with systemic questions has allowed us to recognize that today's choices can shape the future of our organizations.

In this journey, you have learned that systemic questions are not just a tool but a mindset that can enrich the professional practice of managers, coaches, and consultants. They have provided you with the tools to tackle complex challenges, promote growth, and create profound and lasting changes in our organizations.

For anyone aspiring to become a successful leader, coach, or consultant in an increasingly complex and interconnected world, these skills in asking systemic questions and systemic thinking represent a significant competitive advantage. Now is the time to put these lessons into practice, to explore the world of systemic questions, and harness their potential to lead your team, create value, and contribute to the lasting success of your organization. It is an invitation to begin this fascinating journey where systemic thinking and the questions that fuel it await to enrich your professional practice and guide you toward extraordinary results.

Invitation to Apply What You've Learned

After this deep dive into systemic questions, you have gained valuable knowledge and powerful tools that can transform your approach to management, coaching, and consulting. Now is the time to put everything you've learned into practice. Systemic questions represent a key to a world of opportunities where you can confidently address complex challenges, explore organizational dynamics with fresh eyes, and create profound and lasting changes. We invite you to take the helm of your professional growth and apply these skills in your daily life.

You will become a more effective leader, a more empathetic coach, and a more enlightened consultant thanks to what you've learned in this book. Harness the power of systemic questions to lead your team wisely, create value for your organization, and shape the future with a long-term perspective. Don't wait any longer. Begin this new chapter of your career with the awareness that you have unique tools at your disposal. Explore the world of systemic questions and discover how they can enrich your professional practice. With dedication and commitment, you will achieve extraordinary results.

Additional Resources

Recommended Readings

We also recommend five excellent readings for managers who wish to delve deeper into systemic questions and improve their leadership skills in leading a team:

"The Fifth Discipline" by Peter M. Senge

This book is a classic in organizational management and introduces the concept of "systemic thinking" in depth. Senge explains how to apply systemic thinking to address organizational challenges and create successful teams and organizations.

"Humble Inquiry: The Gentle Art of Asking Instead of Telling" by Edgar H. Schein

Edgar Schein, one of the leading experts in leadership and organizational culture, explores the importance of open questions and active listening in managerial contexts. This book offers valuable insights into how to use questions to create meaningful connections and drive change.

"Change Your Questions, Change Your Life" by Marilee G. Adams

Marilee Adams introduces the concept of the "Choice Map," illustrating how the questions we ask ourselves and others can influence our perception and actions. This book provides a practical approach to improving the quality of your questions and interactions.

"The Coaching Habit: Say Less, Ask More & Change the Way You Lead Forever" by Michael Bungay Stanier

Michael Bungay Stanier presents seven essential questions that every manager can use to become a more effective coach. This book provides practical guidance on how to use questions to develop your team's potential.

"Questions Are the Answer: A Breakthrough Approach to Your Most Vexing Problems at Work and in Life" by Hal Gregersen

Hal Gregersen offers a comprehensive overview of the power of questions in problem-solving. He explores how questions can be used to stimulate innovation, improve collaboration, and solve complex problems.

These books cover a wide range of topics related to systemic questions, leadership, and improving management skills. I hope you find these readings helpful in your professional development journey.

Useful Websites and Online Resources

Also, draw inspiration from some websites and online resources useful for managers wishing to delve into systemic questions and improve their leadership skills in leading a team, such as:

The Society for Organizational Learning (SoL):

SoL Website

SoL is a global community of professionals who share knowledge about systemic thinking and organizational learning practices. Their website offers resources, webinars, and publications for exploring systemic thinking in organizations.

Systems Thinker:

Systems Thinker Website

Systems Thinker is an online resource that provides articles, case studies, and practical tools for understanding and applying systemic thinking in management and leadership.

Center for Systems Awareness (CSA):

CSA Website

CSA focuses on systemic awareness and offers online courses, webinars, and resources for developing skills in systemic thinking and action.

Harvard Business Review (HBR):

HBR Section on Systemic Thinking

HBR offers a collection of articles and case studies on systemic thinking, with a focus on practical application in business contexts.

MIT Sloan School of Management - Sustainability Initiative:

Sustainability Initiative

This initiative offers a range of resources, webinars, and publications on systemic thinking applied to sustainability and responsible business management.

Coursera and edX:

Platforms like Coursera (Coursera) and edX (edX) offer online courses on systemic thinking, leadership, and organizational management, including many high-quality university courses.

LinkedIn Learning:

LinkedIn Learning

LinkedIn Learning offers a wide range of online courses on leadership, systemic thinking, and management skills.

YouTube:

Search for videos and lectures on systemic thinking, organizational management, and systemic questions. Many organizations and professionals share informative content on YouTube.

Blogs and Forums:

Explore blogs and forums dedicated to systemic thinking and leadership. You can find insightful discussions and share experiences with other professionals.

Be sure to explore these online resources to deepen your understanding of systemic questions and improve your leadership skills in the managerial context.

Index of Terms

Alphabetical list of key terms used in the book:

Change Management; 18; 19; 22; 65; 66

Change Management; 18; 62; 66

Change Management; 61; 79; 80

Circular Cause And Effect; 8

Circular Thinking; 8; 90

Collaboration; 11; 24; 27; 30; 35; 36; 39; 40; 44; 48; 52; 57; 58; 59; 60; 68; 70; 94

Collaboration; 54

Effective Communication; 16; 18; 69; 70

Effective Communication; 55; 57; 68; 71

Effective Communication; 55

Feedback; 8; 15; 19; 22; 23; 54; 56; 60; 70; 89

Feedback; 86; 87; 89

Interconnection; 10; 13; 23; 26; 28; 37; 38; 78; 88

Interconnection; 89

Internal Dynamics; 24; 25; 34; 35; 39

Key Questions; 20

Key Questions; 20

Leadership; 6; 12; 15; 21; 28; 29; 30; 37; 40; 41; 44; 46; 48; 62; 67; 68; 69; 70; 71; 74; 81; 82; 84; 87; 88; 89; 93; 94; 95; 96

Leadership; 28; 42; 67; 81

Managerial Coaching; 6; 13; 14; 16

Managerial Coaching; 13; 14

Managerial Coaching; 13

Organizational Analysis; 23

Organizational Change; 9; 22; 26; 41; 61; 62; 80

Organizational Change; 61

Organizational Consulting; 6; 11; 16; 32

Organizational Consulting; 32

Organizational Learning; 94

Organizational Learning; 94

Organizational System; 14; 15

Organizational System; 14

Practical Exercises; 7; 87

Practical Exercises; 87

Practical Exercises; 87

Problem-Solving; 6; 29; 48; 49; 50; 51; 52; 53; 70; 73; 90; 94

Solution Identification; 35; 36

Solution Identification; 35

Successful Teams; 29; 30; 93

Successful Teams; 29
Sustainability; 9; 19; 33; 41; 62; 65; 81; 82; 83; 84; 85; 95
Sustainability; 62; 82; 83; 84; 85; 95
Systemic Dialogue; 21; 22
Systemic Dialogue; 21; 22
Systemic Dialogue; 21

Systemic Perspective; 9; 10; 23; 24; 29; 30; 32
Systemic Perspective; 9; 23
Systemic Thinking; 6; 7; 8; 28; 88; 89; 91; 93; 94; 95; 96
Systemic Thinking; 88; 89
Systemic Thinking; 29; 88; 95

These terms represent key concepts discussed in the book and are essential for understanding and successfully applying systemic questions in the context of business management and managerial coaching.

Printed in Great Britain
by Amazon

41997118R00056